TIGER WOODS

CLASSIC PHOTOGRAPHY
BY JULES ALEXANDER

IN BLACK & WHITE

COMMENTARY BY
JOHNNY MILLER

ESSAYS BY

JIM NANTZ — *CBS Sports Commentator*

DAVE ANDERSON — *Columnist, The New York Times*

JAMES DODSON — *Author, "Ben Hogan, An American Life"*

DAMON HACK — *Senior Writer, Sports Illustrated*

LORNE RUBENSTEIN — *Author, "A Season in Dornoch"*

PRODUCED AND DESIGNED BY

HASAK INC.

PUBLISHED BY

ALEXANDER IMAGES, INC.

55 Appleby Road

Bedford, NY 10506

914.967.8985

www.julesalexander.com

Email: aleximages@aol.com

PRODUCED AND DESIGNED BY

HASAK INC.

242 Royal Palm Beach Blvd.

Royal Palm Beach, FL 33414

561.296.3404

Art Director: Larry Hasak

Publishing Consultant: W. Alan Vandenburgh

Editor: Debbie Falcone

Design: Eric Guenette • Prepress: Matthew Ellis

Associate Designer: Amy Hillberg • Production Manager: Erin Rodgers

www.hasak.com

Library of Congress Control Number: 2009923312

ISBN: 978-1-60743-352-1

CONTENTS

2002 U.S. OPEN CHAMPIONSHIP, 15TH TEE, BLACK COURSE; BETHPAGE STATE PARK, FARMINGDALE, NEW YORK

2005 PGA CHAMPIONSHIP, 4TH HOLE, LOWER COURSE; BALTUSROL GOLF CLUB, SPRINGFIELD, NEW JERSEY

PREFACE:
FOCUSED

PHOTOGRAPHERS HAVE an obligation to present our subjects in a positive light, regardless of the circumstances. A photograph can last a lifetime, displayed on a wall, a desk, in an album, or on a computer screen for all the world to see, so it had better be a good one.

As digital photography begins to replace film, I am reminded of some early film camera photographers like Henri Cartier-Bresson, W. Eugene Smith, Robert Capa, and Alfred Eisenstaedt, who roamed the world with just one Leica camera and a single lens, and yet took such magnificent pictures. Unlike all of the accessories available to today's photographers, being unburdened by too much equipment kept these photographers from missing the perfect moment.

I have been blessed to have traveled the world myself, camera strapped around my neck, ready to shoot something, someone, or some image that called out to me. As a young person with my very first camera, I could feel the excitement that photography could provide: looking through the viewfinder of the camera, waiting for the exact moment to capture an image that would be gone in an instant, and then later watching as that image came to life as if by magic in the developer tray. That is what photography is all about. That is what keeps me going.

After a tour in the U.S. Navy serving as an aerial reconnaissance photographer, I returned to New York, where I had begun my photography career, and began shooting photos for the advertising and fashion worlds, which eventually led to my present work in golf.

My very first golf photographs were of Ben Hogan, a great but completely accidental choice. It was in June of 1959, and I was in my studio in New York City reading about

Mr. Hogan playing in the U.S. Open at Winged Foot Golf Club in Mamaroneck, N.Y., about 20 minutes away. I decided to take the train up, head for the golf course with a few cameras, and see what happened, though I didn't have any press credentials. Once at Winged Foot, I found Hogan practicing his bunker shots. I had photographed a lot of famous people in my career, from actors to athletes, but Ben Hogan was different. There was something about him that called out to me, and I decided to make him my self-assignment.

TECHNICAL

Early Tiger Woods pictures were taken with a Nikon camera and black and white Tri-X film. Film was developed in Kodak D-76 developer for 7-8 minutes at 68 degrees.

Prints were made on a Leica Focomat Autofocus 35mm enlarger. The printing paper used was Kodak Fine-Art double-weight glossy dried matte or Ilford Multigrade IV Fiber Paper. Prints were developed in Kodak Dektol by Jules Alexander.

Sequence pictures were created with the Canon EOS series, a device that can shoot as many as 10-12 frames per second, along with a choice of 24-105mm, 180mm, and 300mm lenses, and 1.4 extenders.

Over the next three to four days, I walked with Hogan during practice rounds and on tournament days. As I looked at him in his tan trousers, white shirt, white cap, and black shoes, I decided that there was no way to shoot him except with black and white film. The photographs that I shot during those early summer days in 1959 became the basis for the book *The Hogan Mystique*, published in 1994. Upon publication of the book, I received a very kind letter from Mr. Hogan. In it he said, "Thank you for doing your fabulous photographs. It is one of the finest books I have seen. You have made me fortunate to be your subject."

Almost 50 years later I found myself at another U.S. Open, this one at Torrey Pines in San Diego. Unlike the equipment I used in 1959 following Ben Hogan, I used a digital camera with a silent mode and telephoto lens in 2008. But as in 1959, I was following another legendary golfer: Tiger Woods. And, as I did all those years ago, I chose black and white film to capture the images of Tiger. This book, *Tiger Woods In Black & White*, is a collection of some of the photographs I have shot of Tiger in competition over the last seven years.

Tiger will win more tournaments, set more records, and inspire more people throughout the world. This project has been one of my proudest achievements photographically, and it is my sincere wish that you enjoy my work.

—Jules Alexander, 2009

2001 BUICK CLASSIC, 3RD HOLE, WEST COURSE; WESTCHESTER COUNTRY CLUB, HARRISON, NEW YORK

FOREWORD:
THE BEGINNING

T WAS A STEAMY AUGUST AFTERNOON IN 2000. My old friend Jules Alexander and I had just finished a friendly golf match at the Round Hill Club, the venerable Walter Travis-designed course in Greenwich, Connecticut. As we cooled down on the veranda overlooking the 18th green, Jules proclaimed his intention to "do a book on Tiger Woods," and stated further that he was looking for a partner. Having great respect for Jules' remarkable photographic abilities, not to mention his love of golf and his courtly, always proper manner, I immediately extended my hand, saying, "You just found your partner." We shook hands and began the fun journey leading, nearly nine years later, to *Tiger Woods In Black & White*.

Jules did the heavy lifting, traveling to over fifty golf tournaments, finding the right spots on each course, and waiting endlessly to catch Tiger at the right moment. Patience, I came to learn, is the key to both great photography and to book publishing.

Tiger Woods In Black & White, in many ways, is a bookend to a remarkable career. In 1959, Jules captured Ben Hogan in black and white film at the U.S. Open at Winged Foot, leading to his epoch book *The Hogan Mystique*.

Jules, now eighty-two years young, frequently shoots below his age, swims one thousand yards several days a week, and retains the energy and stamina of a much younger man. Now fifty years later, he has captured the essence of arguably the greatest golfer of all time. In *Tiger Woods In Black & White*, Jules' goal was to capture the grace, power, and intensity of Tiger's game. But he went even further to chronicle his humor, his humanity, and his constant pursuit of perfection.

In bringing together many of the great golf writers of our era, we have sought to complete the picture, to give a broader view of this remarkable man, his prodigious accomplishments, and his rich and complex persona.

We like the picture we have crafted. We hope you will enjoy it, too. As Jim Nantz so eloquently states, Tiger is "a man for the ages."

—*Michael Ainslie, 2009*

OPPOSITE PAGE: 2008 ACCENTURE MATCH PLAY CHAMPIONSHIP, 1ST HOLE; THE GALLERY AT DOVE MOUNTAIN, MARANA, ARIZONA

2005 PGA CHAMPIONSHIP, 18TH HOLE, LOWER COURSE; BALTUSROL GOLF CLUB, SPRINGFIELD, NEW JERSEY

A WIN FOR THE AGES

BY JIM NANTZ

WHAT ELSE COULD ONE POSSIBLY say on April 13, 1997, as Tiger Woods holed his final record-breaking putt on the 72nd green, dismantling all of the hallowed marks at the Masters? On that storied Sunday, Tiger shot a 3-under-par 69 to finish at 18-under par—with a twelve-stroke margin of victory—and became the youngest golfer, at 21 years, 3 months, and 14 days, to win this famed tournament.

Golf has never been the same. Some of us saw it coming years in advance. Having been fortunate enough to "follow the sun" and cover golf tournaments coast to coast, we were already in awe of Tiger's remarkable run through the amateur ranks and his subsequent blistering beginning as a PGA Tour professional.

But it was on golf's grandest stage, Augusta National Golf Club, where Tiger truly stepped up and delivered a performance that was so virtuous, even the fringe fan realized he had done something that transcended the parameters of his sport.

A number of people have reiterated how Tiger's Augusta onslaught introduced golf to a whole new world. And while it is undeniable that Tiger's ethnicity and excellence created a following the sport never had before, it also should be noted that Tiger popularized golf for all audiences. Young and old. Black and white. Asian and American, and beyond. A true champion of the people. A uniter.

OPPOSITE PAGE: 1995 U.S. OPEN CHAMPIONSHIP; SHINNECOCK HILLS GOLF CLUB, SOUTHAMPTON, NEW YORK

Tiger conquered Augusta in 1997 and has never looked back. He is the world's most recognized and respected athlete. His obsession to break all of Jack Nicklaus' records has never wavered. Herein lies the reason Tiger is timeless when it comes to being a role model for every professional athlete today—and for generations to come. Clearly on his way to becoming the first billionaire athlete on the planet, his tenacity has never been compromised. His undying thirst to be the best will never be quenched until major championship number nineteen is in his possession.

It has been a privilege to broadcast Tiger's most "shining moment." At times, he has made my job difficult, as the reservoir of superlatives has run dry. How many different ways can you describe and document his unbelievable achievements?

I have come to the conclusion that the line I uttered from a greenside tower in Augusta on a late Sunday a dozen years ago could have just as easily been, "A Man for the Ages!"

ABOVE: 2005 PGA CHAMPIONSHIP, PRACTICE ROUND, 18TH HOLE, LOWER COURSE;
BALTUSROL GOLF CLUB, SPRINGFIELD, NEW JERSEY

BUTCH HARMON WITH TIGER ON THE PRACTICE TEE.

TIGER WOODS

TIGER WOODS' DETERMINATION

BY DAVE ANDERSON

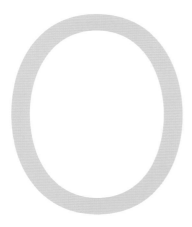N SATURDAY of the 2002 British Open at Muirfield, Tiger Woods' bid for a Grand Slam had disappeared in the wind and the rain and the cold. With the slanting Scottish squalls off the Firth of Forth creating a thirty-nine-degree wind chill, he had soared to a 10-over-par 81—his highest tournament score as a professional golfer.

"It was just blowing so hard out there, it was just difficult to stand," he said that Saturday. "The ball is oscillating. The rain is blowing. On top of that, I just hit poor shots."

At eleven strokes off the lead and trailing sixty-five other golfers, Tiger Woods would have been excused if he had just chosen to go through the motions in Sunday's round. But that's not Tiger Woods' way. Even with Sunday's sunny, warm weather, he knew he probably could not win. And yet he was determined to try. A birdie at the 15th hole put him six strokes off the lead. As he stood on the 16th tee, he had still not surrendered.

"If I could've gone 2-3-3," he said later, "I might've had a chance."

That's Tiger. Always looking ahead, never looking back. Always up, never down. Always positive, never negative.

Always determined to try to somehow find a way to win.

As it turned out, if he had finished birdie-eagle-birdie for what would have been a 61, a record for a major championship, he would have had a chance. With a 61, he would have been 4-under par for the tournament—only two strokes from turning what was a four-man playoff involving Ernie Els, Thomas Levet, Steve Elkington, and Stuart Appleby, into a five-man playoff.

Instead, Tiger finished par-par-par for a 65, a sixteen-stroke difference from the day before and only six strokes out of the playoff (won by Els).

But for Woods even to think of that improbable birdie-eagle-birdie finish on three of the toughest finishing holes in golf provided a peek into his inner determination—the determination to never surrender, to never simply go through the motions, to never dishonor yourself, to always try. The same determination to win the 2008 U.S. Open despite the searing pain in his severely damaged left knee and shin bone. And now the determination to be as good, if not better than before, on his surgically scarred left knee.

Asked before that Open at Torrey Pines if his knee was fully recovered for what would be his first tournament only eight weeks after arthroscopic surgery to repair cartilage following his second-place finish in the Masters, he replied, "Probably not."

Knowing the chronic problems he's had with that knee, his more honest answer might have been, "definitely not." As a child, he injured it skateboarding. As a Stanford freshman in late 1994, he had two benign tumors and scar tissue removed. In December 2002 he had benign cysts and fluid removed. Shortly after having finished tied for 12th in the 2007 British Open at Carnoustie, he was running on a golf course near his Florida home when a misstep ruptured the already weakened anterior cruciate ligament that connects the thigh bone to the shin bone. The injury did not hinder him from winning ten of his next thirteen events, including the PGA Championship at Southern Hills in Tulsa, Oklahoma, but during his intense rehab and zealous preparation for the U.S. Open at Torrey Pines following the April surgery, he developed a double stress fracture of his shin bone. Doctors recommended he use crutches for three weeks, then rest for three more weeks, and forget about the Open. But he was determined.

"I'm playing," he told his doctors, "and I'm winning."

Whenever he winced, grimaced, limped, or turned a golf club into a cane at Torrey

Pines, he was hurting. But somehow he created an 18-hole playoff against Rocco Mediate, with a career-defining 12-foot birdie putt on the 72nd hole, and then won the playoff the next day on the 19th hole after a 4-foot birdie putt on the 18th. Two days later he announced that he needed surgery; a tendon from his right thigh was grafted to replace the torn ligament. As for the stress fractures, his doctors believed they would heal during his recuperation from the knee surgery.

"Sports isn't usually kind to the body," he said after his third U.S. Open victory and fourteenth major championship. "But it's about dealing with it, and getting up there, and giving it your best, and see what happens. And there's never any excuses. You just go play."

Just go play and be determined to win, either coming from behind in pain, as he did at Torrey Pines, or making sure to hold a lead, as he did in the final round of the 2007 PGA Championship at Southern Hills after his three-putt bogey on the 14th hole narrowed his advantage over Woody Austin to one stroke. Going to the next tee, he told himself, "You got

ROCCO MEDIATE AND TIGER SHARE A LAUGH DURING THE TROPHY PRESENTATION CEREMONY AT
THE 2008 U.S. OPEN CHAMPIONSHIP AT TORREY PINES.

yourself into this mess, now earn your way out." Notice the word *earn*. He wasn't assuming or hoping that Austin would make a mistake. He was determined to make a birdie to lengthen his lead. On the next hole, he made that birdie with a 15-foot putt for what would be the winning two-stroke margin.

"I knew what I had to do when I'm in that situation; I know what it takes," he had said the evening before when reminded that he had always won after holding or sharing the fifty-four-hole lead in twelve previous majors. "There's a certain feel that you get out there that you can understand what the guys could do and are capable of doing."

This determination was implanted in Tiger Woods by his late father, Earl. In the foreword of his father's 1998 book, *Playing Through: Straight Talk On Hard Work, Big Dreams and Adventures with Tiger*, he writes how his Pop "had the fortitude and determination to be the best he could be in spite of resistance at so many steps along the way." And long before the world knew him as Tiger, young Eldrick Woods developed the determination to always try to do his best, to always try to improve, to always try to shape a better swing. The determination to win. And as he recuperated from knee-ligament surgery, the determination to be as dominating as ever.

Tiger's not alone. In golf, Jack Nicklaus, Ben Hogan, and Bobby Jones had that determination. So did Michael Jordan in basketball, Johnny Unitas in football, Muhammad Ali in boxing, Joe DiMaggio in baseball.

Before a hot and humid doubleheader, DiMaggio once mentioned how he looked forward to playing that day. Asked how he could enjoy both games in sweltering weather, he said, "Maybe somebody never saw me before."

That's the determination to always perform at your best. The same determination that Tiger Woods displayed in making a PGA Tour record of 142 consecutive cuts, or 147 if you don't count his failure to return in August to the rescheduled 1998 AT&T Pebble Beach National Pro-Am that began the previous February, or 111 if you just count the tournaments in which there was no cut.

Whatever number you prefer, it reflects the determination that he needed to survive several close calls, such as having been two strokes above the projected cut with only six holes to play in the 2004 PGA Championship at Whistling Straits.

"I had to somehow just grind it out and be patient, and hopefully, things would come around. And they did," he said after he birdied the 13th, 16th, and 17th holes for a 69, one stroke under the cut. "I try as hard as I can. I've always done that. I think that's one thing I'm most proud of, that I've never bagged it."

Tiger had that determination long before he burst onto the PGA Tour, long before his teenage streak of winning three U.S. Junior Amateur titles and then three U.S. Amateur Championships.

At the 2000 British Open he told of how, as a golf wunderkind, he showed his determination while playing two holes with Sam Snead in an exhibition near Los Angeles.

"I was five or six," he said. "Sam had a new group of playing partners every two holes, and I got a chance to play with him the last two. I couldn't carry this little par 3 with a creek in front, so I was trying to bounce it on the cart path through the creek. I missed it. My dad says it missed by a few yards to the right. It rolled into a rocky creek. I got in there to play it. The ball was sitting up. From behind me, Sam yells, 'What are you doing?' I look around, look dumbfounded. I'm going to hit the shot. He says, 'Just pick it up and drop it. Let's go on.' I didn't like that very much. I remember looking at my ball and saying, 'I've got to hit it. I don't want to drop. That's a penalty.' So I hit a 7-iron onto the green, all wet, two-putted, got my bogey, and bogeyed the last. I made bogey-bogey and Sam beat me by two—par, par."

Tiger's determination had already emerged, even at that young age, along with his desire to play his ball out of the rocky creek even as Sam Snead, golf's ageless wonder who was 68 or 69 at the time, suggested he pick it up.

That same determination was there at Augusta National in 1997 in Tiger's first Masters as a pro. The year before, after the Stanford sophomore enjoyed a practice round with Jack Nicklaus and Arnold Palmer, the Golden Bear told reporters, "Arnold and I agreed that Tiger's going to win as many Masters as Arnold and I together."

That would be ten Masters—six for Nicklaus, four for Palmer.

But through seven holes of his first Masters as a pro, Tiger was struggling. Then his tee shot on the 535-yard uphill 8th hole hooked wildly into the pine trees and stopped close to a cart path. Disdaining a drop and with the spikes of his right shoe grinding into the cart-path pavement and his left shoe straddling the rounded curb, he punched a 6-iron between two small trees onto the fairway. He salvaged a bogey, but when he walked off the 9th green, he had gone out in 4-over-par 40.

"I was pretty hot going to the 10th tee," he said later. "I couldn't keep the ball in the fairway. I couldn't attack the pin. I knew what I was doing wrong. I was in such a bad position at the top of the backswing, I was coming off the ball."

At age twenty, in the middle of the first round of his first Masters as a pro, Tiger not only determined what he had been doing wrong, he was determined to correct it. On the back nine, he shot a 6-under-par 30 that included a 151-yard wedge to four feet that positioned an eagle 3 on the 15th hole. Over the years there have been hundreds of 70s recorded in the Masters, but his 70 that day is the only one carved with 40-30, a 10-stroke drop from the front nine to the back nine. And that back-nine 30 propelled him to his first Masters green jacket and his first major.

Other majors followed, notably his walkover in the 2000 U.S. Open at Pebble Beach when he won by fifteen strokes with a record 12-under par and, a month later, an eight-stroke victory at St. Andrews in the 2000 British Open.

In the 2000 PGA Championship at Valhalla Golf Club outside Louisville, Kentucky, his determination proved to be the difference. After a 70 in Saturday's third round, he had a one-stroke lead on lesser-knowns Bob May and Scott Dunlap, but he returned to the practice range and then stayed on the putting green until it was too dark to even see the hole.

"I worked on my swing and my putting," he said. "I tried to feel a little more steady over the ball and let the toe of the blade release a little better."

But on the tee of the par-5 18th hole in the final round, he suddenly realized that he

needed a birdie, either to win or to force a playoff with May.

"Par wasn't going to get it done," he said. "The way the day had been going, I expected Bob to make that putt on 18, so when he made it, I had to make mine [a five-foot putt]. That is the mental preparation for it. To step up there and play that putt—a ball outside the left from a short distance like that, and know that you have to trust your stroke and the break and stay committed. When it goes in, it really feels pretty good."

After the putt went in, Tiger won the three-hole playoff with May by one stroke, 12 to 13. Early in 2001 he won the Masters for his fourth consecutive major title—the only pro golfer ever to accomplish that feat.

Tiger suddenly had all four major trophies on the coffee table of his home in the Isleworth enclave outside Orlando, Florida—the Tiger Slam as some people called it, not a Grand Slam of the four majors in the same calendar year, as purists called it. But he was justifiably proud of what he had done.

"I think the harder way to accomplish a Grand Slam is in one year," he said, "but if

ABOVE: LINING UP A PUTT ON THE 16TH GREEN AT MUIRFIELD VILLAGE GOLF CLUB AT
THE 2007 MEMORIAL TOURNAMENT

you can put all four trophies on your coffee table, I think you can make a pretty good case for that too."

With his victory in the 2002 U.S. Open at Bethpage Black, he had won six of his last nine majors before the chill wind and rain of Muirfield in the 2002 British Open ended his opportunity for a Grand Slam in one calendar year. But in his next major, the 2002 PGA at Hazeltine, outside Minneapolis, his determination flared again late in the final round. One of sport's oldest truths is that if you want to see a great athlete at his best, see him or her when they're getting beat. And on the back nine of that PGA's final round, Tiger was getting beat. He had bogeyed both the 13th and 14th holes to fall behind Rich Beem, but as he walked down the fairway of the 586-yard 15th hole, he turned to his caddie Steve Williams.

"If we birdie in, we'll win the tournament," Tiger said. "Let's just suck it up and get it done."

"If we birdie in." As if it were as simple as that. And in his determination, Tiger did just that, but Beem held him off, winning by a stroke. Tiger was annoyed at himself for those two

ABOVE: TIGER'S PRACTICE ROUTINE RESEMBLES THAT OF YEAR'S PAST (SEE PHOTO ON PAGE 10)

earlier bogeys that ended up meaning the difference between winning and finishing second.

"But I'm also pretty jacked up at the way I played coming in," he said after that final round. "That's something I'm proud of. I could have easily just bagged it and made pars, but that's not the way I play."

The way Tiger plays is by being determined to win, even when he's getting beaten. That was never more evident than in the 2005 Masters. In their final-round duel, Chris DiMarco was three strokes better, 68 to 71, forcing a sudden-death playoff. But on the first playoff hole, No. 18, Tiger drilled a 3-wood into the center of the fairway, then lofted an 8-iron about fifteen feet above the hole, and sank the birdie putt for his fourth green jacket.

"I just tried to hang in there," he said. "In the playoff, I hit two of the best golf shots I hit all week. It was pretty sweet. The 3-wood was perfect and the 8-iron I hit in there was flush. I made a nice little putt there too."

Three months later at the 2005 British Open at St. Andrews, he made another nice little putt when he needed one. During the third round, his lead had been shaved to one stroke over José Maria Olazábal, and then, on the 17th green, he needed a ten-foot putt for par. After taking more time than usual to study the line, he putted his ball, watched it disappear into the cup, and, with a smile, hurried to snatch it. He had remained at par for the round, and when his putt from 150 feet on the 18th rolled and rolled and finally crawled to a stop for a tap-in birdie, he took a two-stroke lead into Sunday and won by four strokes.

But it was his determination to make that putt on the 17th in Saturday's round that had turned him towards his tenth major title.

"If I missed that putt," he said, "I would go back to over par, and I'd have to birdie 18 to get back to level par. Just to work that hard and have to birdie 18 to get back to even par, I couldn't see that happening. So might as well make the putt and birdie 18 to finish under par."

Tiger Woods couldn't see that happening. His determination would not allow him to see it. His determination was what made the difference in winning that British Open. It has made the difference in everything. His determination has made him who he is.

2005 PGA CHAMPIONSHIP, 4TH TEE, LOWER COURSE; BALTUSROL GOLF CLUB, SPRINGFIELD, NEW JERSEY

METHODS OF THE MASTER

COMMENTARY BY JOHNNY MILLER

In 1993, I traveled with my son, Scott, to Portland, Oregon, to watch him play in the U.S. Junior Amateur at Waverley Country Club. On the eve of the championship, officials conducted a long-driving contest. The idea was to see if anyone could drive the ball over the yawning Willamette River, which runs along the course. To reach the far bank looked all but impossible and sure enough, none of the first kids who stepped up were able to reach the far bank. Then Tiger Woods approached the tee.

At age 17, Tiger already was fairly well-known. He had won two U.S. Juniors already and was trying for an unprecedented third in a row. Tiger made a swing with the driver that made everyone gasp, and they then fell silent as the ball almost disappeared from sight. The ball not only carried the river, it flew the small shoreline and disappeared into a rise above the bank. It was an awesome display of power, and though my attention that week was focused on Scott, I also was mesmerized by Tiger. I've been fascinated with Tiger and his game ever since, and through my announcing work at NBC Sports, I've followed his career as closely as anyone.

As I pore over Jules Alexander's remarkable action photographs of Tiger taken at various stages of his career, I have to remind myself that his game is still a work in progress.

THE ADJACENT PHOTO OF TIGER IS REMINISCENT OF A PHOTOGRAPH JULES ALEXANDER CAPTURED OF JOHNNY MILLER, INSET, WHICH APPEARED ON THE COVER OF *GOLF MAGAZINE* IN MARCH OF 1982

Tiger's golf swing is an evolving thing that has had several distinct stages. There was the powerful, feel-oriented swing I saw at Waverley. Then came the influence of Butch Harmon and the more refined technique he used early in his pro career, what I call his "first prime." Next there was a transition period where Tiger struggled a bit (but still won tournaments) as he sought to incorporate the philosophy of instructor Hank Haney. Then there is the swing we see today, in Tiger's "second prime." Only time will tell where his game will go from here, and what it might look like 10 years from now. It's a fascinating thing to imagine.

Jules' photos provide us with telling glimpses of Tiger at important stages of his pro career, and give us tremendous insight into the technical side of perhaps the greatest golfer in history. As I write this, Tiger has yet to break Jack Nicklaus' record of eighteen professional majors, so "greatest" does come with that caveat. But there's no question in my mind that Tiger at his best would beat Jack at his best, and that satisfies many people's criteria as to which player is better.

The reader can learn a lot from examining the photographs and my accompanying comments, for Tiger is the most mechanically sound golfer ever. But I warn you, there are limits. Tiger's swing is not effective merely because of his textbook positions and execution. He has extraordinary strength and flexibility; phenomenal speed in his hands, arms, and torso; superb balance; a vivid imagination and total concentration; and tremendous awareness of where the club is in relation to his body. You can improve your game by watching Tiger, but you will never be Tiger any more than you'll become Kobe Bryant by watching him on video and then shooting baskets in your driveway.

Perhaps the best thing to do is simply pour a cold drink, sit back and admire this great athlete in action. Tiger Woods is that once-in-a-lifetime genius whose style can be copied, but never duplicated. We're lucky to live in his time, and to have Jules' photographs for posterity.

GOLD-MEDAL FLEXIBILITY

Tiger is gifted with uncommonly strong, wide shoulders. It's not a trait the average golfer should envy necessarily, because well-muscled shoulders can constrict the shoulder turn, both back and through. But Tiger is not an average physical specimen. Just look at the fullness of his follow-through. His left shoulder is behind his right ear, while his right shoulder is in front of his nose. This much flexibility is very rare among male golfers. It's more common on the LPGA Tour—and on the medals podium for Olympic gymnasts.

The finish of the swing reveals a great deal of what went on earlier. In this case, the fact that Tiger's right shoulder is so high reveals he was hitting a high, powerful draw.

INVITATIONS TO POWER

Tiger has always generated ferocious speed and power with the driver and fairway woods. Two sources of his enormous length are evident in the photo at right. First, he has unwound his hips as far as they'll go, while his chest and shoulders are still square to the ball. Second—and this is the move I really love—he's extending his arms tremendously. It's almost like his left arm is ready to leave the shoulder socket. He's created tremendous width, which really fuels his clubhead speed.

Despite all that speed, Tiger shows superb balance deep into his follow-through. His belt buckle is facing left of the target; this is rare. The slight "reverse C" finish shows that he kept the clubhead square well after impact. That gives him some semblance of control to go with all that power.

IN SEARCH OF "RANGER RICK"

Accuracy with the driver has never been Tiger's strong suit, and with his 130 mph clubhead speed, how could it be? Yet he doesn't seem to struggle with wayward driving when he's on the practice tee; he derisively refers to himself as "Ranger Rick" because of his ability to drive the ball string straight in practice. Tiger is not swinging particularly hard in the photo above, and I believe he would be well-served to duplicate this type of physical effort in competition. If he did, he'd enjoy greater accuracy, while still having distance to burn. We'll see if that's how he evolves.

Jules' photo of Tiger on the facing page demonstrates how hard Tiger goes at it with the driver in tournament play. This was shot fairly early in Tiger's pro career, when his power was at its zenith. He was so long back in 1997 and '98 that, had he been able to use the hotter drivers so common today, he'd be as long as anybody on the PGA Tour, J.B. Holmes and Bubba Watson included.

MR. NEUTRAL

Tiger's swing with the irons these days has very little nuance to it. Mechanically it is very

pure, with no dramatic manipulations or "makeup moves" with his body or the golf club.

This iron shot is textbook stuff—a "deep" follow-through with maximum extension, his

left arm not yet beginning to fold. Note how his left elbow is pointing at his left hip; every golfer should copy that. Tiger is swinging less than all-out, otherwise the ball, which is adjacent to caddie Steve Williams' eyes, would have left the frame.

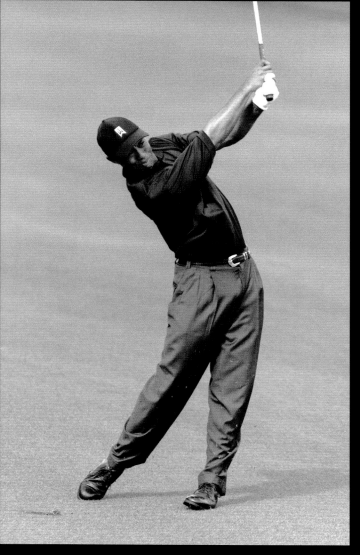

ANATOMY OF A FADE

The high, soft fade is Tiger's bread-and-butter shot, and he's playing it to perfection here. Even though the ball is long gone, note in the photo on the facing page how the clubface is still square to Tiger's hands, much like he surely set everything at address. He's released the club fully, yet it has not rotated closed. His divot is nice and shallow, proof that he's swung from the inside instead of coming down steeply from the outside. He's keeping his head down beautifully, the hallmark of great iron players. His weight shift and footwork are gorgeous, almost like a dancer. His follow-through and finish are terrific, but how could they be anything else?

MASTER FROM TROUBLE

Tiger has never been a particularly straight d
and we've seen him play his second shots fro
some nasty places. But Tiger is one of the gre
trouble-shot players of all time. All the quali
player needs—strength, imagination, the abi
judge his lie, and a knack for controlling traj
and curvature—Tiger has in abundance. The
he's playing here is not particularly confining
it's a cold, wet day, and the grass is a foot hig
He's exhibiting tremendous power and a grea
of control, as evidenced by the clubshaft stay
line with his left forearm. Concentration and
are etched on his face.

ACTIVE HANDS, QUIET BODY

It takes quite a bit of clubhead speed to make the ball "climb the shaft" at such a steep angle. Tiger doesn't seem to be expending any effort at all. How does he do it? The key is his left-hand grip. It's in a strong position, rotated well to Tiger's right, so he can see three knuckles when he looks down at address. The strong grip made it easier to cock his wrists sharply and release the clubhead into the ball with a lot of speed. It's strictly a hands-and-wrists shot; his body is very quiet. In the photo above (a different shot), note how the clubface is still square well after impact. He's made the divot not with the leading edge of the clubface, but with the rear of the flange. Tiger is a master at regulating the loft of the clubface to match the shot, and he's maintained loft beautifully here.

GENIUS AT WORK

You don't need to see Tiger's eyes—he's no doubt looking at the target—to reveal his powers

of concentration, or see his imagination at work. In the photo on the facing page, Tiger is

sizing up a pitch shot and has programmed several elements of the shot. His right knee is

angled forward in preparation for supporting his body during the forward swing. The shaft

angle and clubface position has been established, his grip pressure is light, and all he needs

to do is lower the clubhead behind the ball and pull the trigger.

The photo above again reveals the depth of his imagination. He's obviously off the

green and chipping with a longer club. He's choking down for control, adopting his putting

grip so as to make a one-piece stroke, while maintaining his posture. Tiger is as good a chipper

as the game has ever known, and his willingness to try different shots is one of the things

that set him apart from other players.

SHORT-GAME POWER

In this series of photos, Tiger is demonstrating how strength is a huge asset in the short game. In photo 1 (facing page, top), Tiger has kept the clubface square through impact and beyond, which is enormously hard to do on short shots from deep rough. He's anticipated the tendency for the grass to grab the hosel and twist the clubface closed. The result: A nice shot, and a bale of hay.

In photo 2 (facing page, bottom), he's "riding the horse," having widened his stance and flexed his knees to ensure that he stay down through impact. It takes strength and mental discipline to try to drive the ball low from tall grass, but he's pulled it off. In photo 3 (above), he's again maintaining his knee flex. That poor left knee is taking the brunt of the blow. Ouch!

MAKING THE HARD LOOK EASY

To the average golfer, sand is a true hazard. To a player of Tiger's caliber, basic sand shots like the one he's playing here are fun, a chance to show off a little. Tiger's demeanor in these photos is especially relaxed. There's plenty of green to work

with, the lie obviously is nice and level with the ball sitting up, and there is no special challenge in terms of elevation. It's no surprise that the ball stopped a foot from the hole.

From a mechanics standpoint, note how open the clubface is at the top of his swing and how well he maintains his posture. His body is nice and loose, and he swings through the ball without tension and very little physical effort.

THE ATHLETE PUTTER

Because most of the body is quiet during the putting stroke, it's hard to imagine that athleticism would come into play. But Tiger does it. See how he angles his left foot toward the target? This allows him to swing his arms freely through the ball instead of stopping at impact. Note, too, how his right thumb is placed straight down the shaft. The thumbs are the most sensitive digits on your hand, and his thumb position accentuates his sense of feel. Tiger's putting style has a linear, mechanical quality to it, but there's a lot of art in there, too.

Tiger is a superb green-reader, too. It isn't just his ability to discern small breaks and judge the speed that makes him great. His biggest advantage is his memory. Tiger plays the same courses on tour year after year, and he has an uncanny ability to recall how certain putts behaved in years past. He remembers not only his putts, but those of his fellow competitors as well. Thus, he's very knowledgeable about how water, mountains, and drainage affect the way the ball rolls.

THE AILING LEFT KNEE

At this point, nobody knows exactly how Tiger initially injured his left knee, but I've always suspected that one characteristic of his swing exacerbated the injury. Early in his career especially, Tiger snapped his left leg straight violently through impact. This helped him clear his left hip and no doubt helped generate tremendous clubhead speed, but it also put stress on his knee. I speak from experience, because I also used to snap my left leg straight, and I also had problems with my left knee. It's a sound move mechanically, but demanding physically.

Notice in the photo at left how Tiger's left heel is well off the ground, his pant leg flying from the effort. His knee is absorbing a great deal of the force of the swing, and when you make thousands of swings like that over many years, it's bound to take a toll. One aspect of Tiger's work with Hank Haney is that he doesn't go up on his toes as much as he's doing here. His left heel is much more "grounded" through impact, and there's less stress imparted on that knee. It's an important modification that should add to Tiger's longevity.

MATURATION AS A COMPETITOR
(FOLLOWING PAGES)

Passion, spirit, and determination are Tiger's fifteenth club, and they, too, are worthy of deconstruction. Early in Tiger's career, his fist-pumping celebrations were the most exuberant in golf, and he exhibited them often. As Tiger's career has ripened and his triumphs have multiplied, the celebrations have become less frequent and slightly less demonstrative. He's turned into an experienced, battle-hardened warrior who saves his energy-expending celebrations for the moments that really matter. This putt, one of many that dropped during the final round of the 2008 U.S. Open at Torrey Pines, was one of those moments.

TIGER WOODS:
A PORTRAIT
IN WORDS

BY LORNE RUBENSTEIN

T'S IMPOSSIBLE to take one's eyes off Tiger Woods, as Jules Alexander realized when he started photographing him. Jules had found an ideal subject, as he had in Ben Hogan before. In his compositions, Jules finds what the photographer Henri Cartier-Bresson called the "decisive moment." It is decisive, John Szarkowski wrote in his classic book *The Photographer's Eye*, "not because of the exterior event (the bat meeting the ball) but because in that moment the flux of changing forms and patterns was sensed to have achieved balance and clarity and order—because the image became, for an instant, a *picture.*"

Here we see Tiger, taut at the top of his swing. Here Jules catches Tiger bouncing a ball on his clubface, a moment in time, his mind quiet, all silence, his eyes trained on the task. Here we see Tiger in sand, his lower body almost fixed in place. We see Tiger smiling as kids watch him. They are dazzled. We see him concentrated on the ball as his caddie and trusted partner Steve Williams tosses it to him on a practice range. We see Tiger Woods the golfer, because we see Tiger Woods the human being, engaged in his craft, fully engaged. We see him through Jules' eyes and lens, because Jules sees him.

It was the early spring of 1993, and a skinny teenager who had won the last two U.S. Junior Amateur Championships was on a hillside behind the ninth green at the Weston Hills Country Club in Fort Lauderdale. Tiger Woods was 17, and he was playing the PGA Tour's Honda Classic. This was during a practice round, and Woods was hitting shots from

all sorts of lies. A flop shot. A chunk and run. A low billiards shot off a slope toward the hole. Every few minutes another PGA Tour pro would show up to watch the youngster. Woods was all body language as he watched his shots. He twisted to one side or the other. He rolled his eyes. He raised his head and pursed his lips as a shot just missed the hole. He was putting on a show.

Tiger Woods is both actor and reactor. He is a performer whose skills and instincts have created moments to remember since he first came to our attention. This was during *The Mike Douglas Show*, when he was just two years old. Douglas invited Tiger to the stage, where Bob Hope and Jimmy Stewart waited for him. He walked out briskly, with purpose, a golf bag over his shoulders, accompanied by his father Earl. Tiger hit a ball into a canvas off a tee on the makeshift green that had been set up and held a smile as the club wrapped

ABOVE AND OPPOSITE PAGE: TIGER RECEIVING INSTRUCTION FROM HANK HANEY

2005 PGA CHAMPIONSHIP, PRACTICE ROUND, 6TH HOLE, LOWER COURSE; BALTUSROL GOLF CLUB, SPRINGFIELD, NEW JERSEY

around behind his back. Douglas suggested a putting contest with Bob Hope, and Tiger tried to make a three-foot putt. The ball rolled by the hole. Douglas offered another try, and Tiger's father put the ball down, again three feet from the hole. Tiger picked up the ball and placed it on the edge of the hole. He couldn't miss from there. Hope and Stewart, Hall of Fame actors, got a great kick out of Tiger's move. On stage, he had performed and he had won.

"It's not too often when somebody one-ups him," Tiger said many years later of his upstaging Hope. "But I got him pretty good by moving the ball closer to the hole. I got him pretty good."

More than thirty years later, Tiger continues to perform at the highest levels, and stretches the boundaries of the possible. We chronicle his actions and reactions in words and in photographs, as Jules Alexander does here with such power. We see a golfer who is rarely satisfied. We see a golfer who assesses his play on nearly a shot-by-shot basis, and who evaluates his success by his results in majors. He aspires to playing golf with an ultimate combination of art and science, the objective being to generate control and precision. To follow him closely, as I have since his amateur days when he won U.S. Juniors from 1991-1993 and U.S. Amateurs from 1994-1996, is to observe a golfer who aspires to hitting a perfect shot every time and to making a pure stroke every putt. Tiger's devotion is to one shot, that one shot, his universe distilled into a moment of concentration. Shot by shot, major by major, he approaches Jack Nicklaus' record of eighteen professional major championships. As I write, he has won fourteen of these majors.

As a golf-watcher first, and then a golf writer, I've been fortunate to be around both when Nicklaus was winning majors and during Tiger's entire career. I was a teenager when my father took me to the 1965 Canadian Open at the Mississaugua Golf and Country Club just west of Toronto. Nicklaus was in a battle for the championship with Gene Littler as he played the final holes. Nicklaus, the great Nicklaus, fluffed a shot on the short par-four 17th in the last round, and Littler won. I remember Nicklaus' grace in losing. I realized then that even the champions of the game—the true champions—are vulnerable, even fragile. Golf is difficult. Nobody masters it on every shot.

Twenty-one years later, in 1986, I was in the stands left of the 15th green at the Augusta National Golf Club when Nicklaus struck his magisterial 4-iron within twenty-five feet of the hole in the final round at the Masters, and then made the putt for eagle. I swiveled my head left and watched Nicklaus hit his tee shot at the par-3 16th to within three feet of the hole. Nicklaus' eyesight was such that he couldn't see the ball finish its flight and stop so close to the hole, but that didn't matter. He knew he had hit a quality shot when it counted. The feel of the ball off the clubface told him all he needed to know. Nicklaus bent to pick up his tee as the ball spun out near the hole. He made the birdie putt and went on to win his sixth Masters. Nicklaus was forty-six years old. He had won his eighteenth major.

Nicklaus in those days was often asked whether he thought anybody would one day come along to dominate the game as he had. He said that a golfer would one day arrive who was tall and strong, so that he could develop a long, wide arc and hit the ball great distances. He said this golfer would have won from an early age, so he would be confident when he turned professional. He would have developed the ability to hit just about any shot he wanted, allied to the imagination and inventiveness to create shots as required. He would have a deft short game, and a putting stroke to match. He would have an ideal golfing mind, a love of the game, especially of hitting shots, and a willingness and desire to keep learning. His will would be strong. This fellow would be the complete golfer. Tiger Woods is this golfer.

More than anything, perhaps, it's apparent that Tiger appreciates the simple pleasures of the game. He's like a kid on the driving range when he experiments with shots and his swing, with making something new and different happen even as he tries to become as consistent a player as possible. He becomes most animated, most himself, when he is working on his game, playing with friends such as Mark O'Meara and John Cook in casual rounds, and, of course, when he is competing. He is not only himself, he is within himself, locked into a cocoon of concentration. So narrowly focused, he expands. He finds a way to perform.

It was appropriate, then, that Tiger blossomed so fully into himself during the 1997 Masters. This was eleven years after Nicklaus won his sixth and final Masters, and it was Tiger's first as a professional. He had shot 40 on the front nine. Forty? Tiger Woods? Nicklaus had famously predicted after a practice round with him the year before that he would win more green jackets than he and Arnold Palmer combined. Nicklaus was predicting that Tiger would win the Masters at least eleven times.

OPPOSITE: 2002 PGA CHAMPIONSHIP, HAZELTINE NATIONAL GOLF CLUB, CHASKA, MINNESOTA
FOLLOWING PAGES: 2005 PGA CHAMPIONSHIP, BALTUSROL GOLF CLUB, SPRINGFIELD, NEW JERSEY

Now he was 4-over par after his opening nine holes. He drilled down deeply into himself as he made the short walk from the 9th green to the 10th tee, as he sunk into what he had called in his Tuesday press conference a "totally obsessed state." He added, "I know how to focus. I've done it before."

Tiger concluded that he had been taking the club back too far on the front nine. He needed to tighten things up. He birdied the 10th hole, chipped in for birdie with a 9-iron bump and run—creativity defined—from behind the green on the 12th, birdied the par-5 13th, and eagled the par-5 15th. He birdied the 17th and parred the 18th to shoot 30 on the back nine. He'd shot 40-30. There was then, and this was now. Three days later, Tiger walked up the hill to the 18th green, leading by 12 shots. He left himself with a five-foot putt for par. He hadn't three-putted all week and wanted to maintain that clean slate. The putt went down. He'd finished 18-under-par, setting a new Masters record.

"My focus never left me," he said of how he played the last hole, of his intensity over his last putt.

It never does. Tiger, even when he's practicing, is locked in. Watch him work on the range or during a practice round. His work is play. Fifteen months after Tiger won his first Masters, he won on the range after the third round of the British Open at the Royal Birkdale Golf Club in Southport, England. He had shot 7-over-par 77 in the third round and was five shots behind third-round leader Brian Watts. David Duval was a shot further behind. It was late in the evening, and only Tiger and Duval were on the range. Tiger's then-instructor Butch Harmon was watching him. A couple of hundred spectators were in the stands behind the range, and soon they were urging Tiger and Duval to put on a show. They accepted the invitation, and were soon calling shots before they hit them, and criss-crossing shots in the air. Tiger was again performing. He was enjoying himself. He was practicing. He was playing.

On Sunday, Tiger finished birdie-par-birdie-birdie, and then watched on television as the championship wound down. His 66 put him a shot out of a playoff between Watts and

O'Meara, which O'Meara won. But he had been there at the end, right there. Perhaps it had

something to do with the performance he had put on the night before. He was five shots off

the lead, but he knew it was possible to make up that ground.

Tiger always sees possibilities. He sees a vast array of them in each shot. John Jerome ad-

dressed this sort of vision in his book *The Sweet Spot In Time: The Search For Athletic Perfection.*

He wrote that just as elite musicians can sense more notes between the usual complement, so

can elite athletes distinguish nearly infinite gradations of differences in their own movements.

Tiger can see tiny spaces, he can perceive windows of opportunity in shots, and not only vi-

sualize exactly how he wants to contact the ball, but precisely where he wants it to land. He

connects to specific spots perhaps better than anybody who has played golf. His brilliance is

2008 U.S. OPEN CHAMPIONSHIP, SOUTH COURSE; TORREY PINES GOLF COURSE, LA JOLLA, CALIFORNIA

in seeing and feeling spaces, and then in shaping his swing and body angles so that his shots find them.

"I look at Tiger through the viewfinder, and I see the same look I saw on Hogan's face," Jules says. "I see the same look on Itzhak Perlman when he plays violin, and on [Rudolf] Nureyev when he dances. Great athletes have the look. It's 'I'm the best. I want to win.' They're doing something at such a high level, and it's so easy for them that there's no need to strain. There's something beautiful about it to the camera."

So many moments help us appreciate the qualities that set Tiger apart. Who can forget his accomplishment at Pebble Beach when he won the 2000 U.S. Open? He took an 8-shot lead into the final round, and, clearly, he was not going to lose the championship. Tiger had said the evening before that he'd often held the lead into a final round and was usually able to win from that enviable position. But he added that he still had a job to do. The USGA was not going to give Tiger his first U.S. Open by acclamation.

Still, how would he motivate himself? Bill Bradley, the gifted basketball player who starred for Princeton University before doing the same for the New York Knicks for ten years, had written that it was important to get what he called the "chills" for an upcoming game. Woods needed to find a way to get the chills in the final round at Pebble Beach. He set a goal of playing a bogey-free final round at Pebble, one of the game's most storied courses. No U.S. Open champion had played the final round without a bogey, anywhere, let alone at Pebble.

And yet Tiger was bogey-free when he stood over his approach shot on the par-4, 403-yard 16th hole that memorable Sunday, and 15 shots ahead of Ernie Els, in second place. He and Els were playing in the final twosome. Tiger's shot to the 16th green, with a 9-iron from the first cut of shorter rough, flew at the hole cut in the rear-left portion of the green. But the ball carried too far and finished over the green and in high, thick rough. Woods needed to make sure he would put the ball on the green, so that he would have a putt for par. He took a convincing swing at the ball, popping it out of the rough. The ball rolled fifteen feet by the hole. He made the par putt and gave his caddie and partner Steve Williams a look that

said, "How about that, Stevie? Saved my par." The shot was remarkable for the energy Woods invested in it and the attention he paid. He had the tournament won, but he still had another goal: a bogey-free final round at the U.S. Open. Tiger had a major case of the chills.

Tiger had two holes to play. He hit his tee shot into a bunker left of the green on the par-3 17th hole and focused on getting up-and-down for par. Nothing else mattered at that point.

The champion golfer makes the shots when he needs to make them. Dave Anderson in this book writes that Joe DiMaggio relished the idea of playing a doubleheader one hot and humid day. Why? "Maybe somebody never saw me before," DiMaggio said. Michael Jordan stole the ball near the buzzer of the sixth game in the 1998 NBA final between his Chicago

Bulls and Utah Jazz. His shot won the game and championship. Lance Armstrong won his

seventh consecutive Tour de France in 2005, and then retired from cycling. In his book *Lance*

Armstrong's War, Daniel Coyle writes that he "is fascinating for many reasons, but mostly

because he's our purest embodiment of the fundamental human act—to impose the will on

the uncaring world—an act that compels our attention because it seems too simple and yet

is secretly magical. Because at its core, will is about belief, and with Armstrong we can see

the belief happening."

As Tiger settled into the bunker left of the 17th green at Pebble Beach, it was apparent

that the belief was happening. He planted his feet to stabilize himself on the sidehill,

downhill lie and splashed his ball out so that it landed softly. The ball rolled a couple of

ABOVE: TIGER'S APPROACH SHOT TO THE FINAL HOLE AT THE 2008 ARNOLD PALMER INVITATIONAL.
FOLLOWING PAGES: TIGER'S THIRTY-FIVE FOOT PUTT ON THE 18TH GREEN SECURES HIS VICTORY

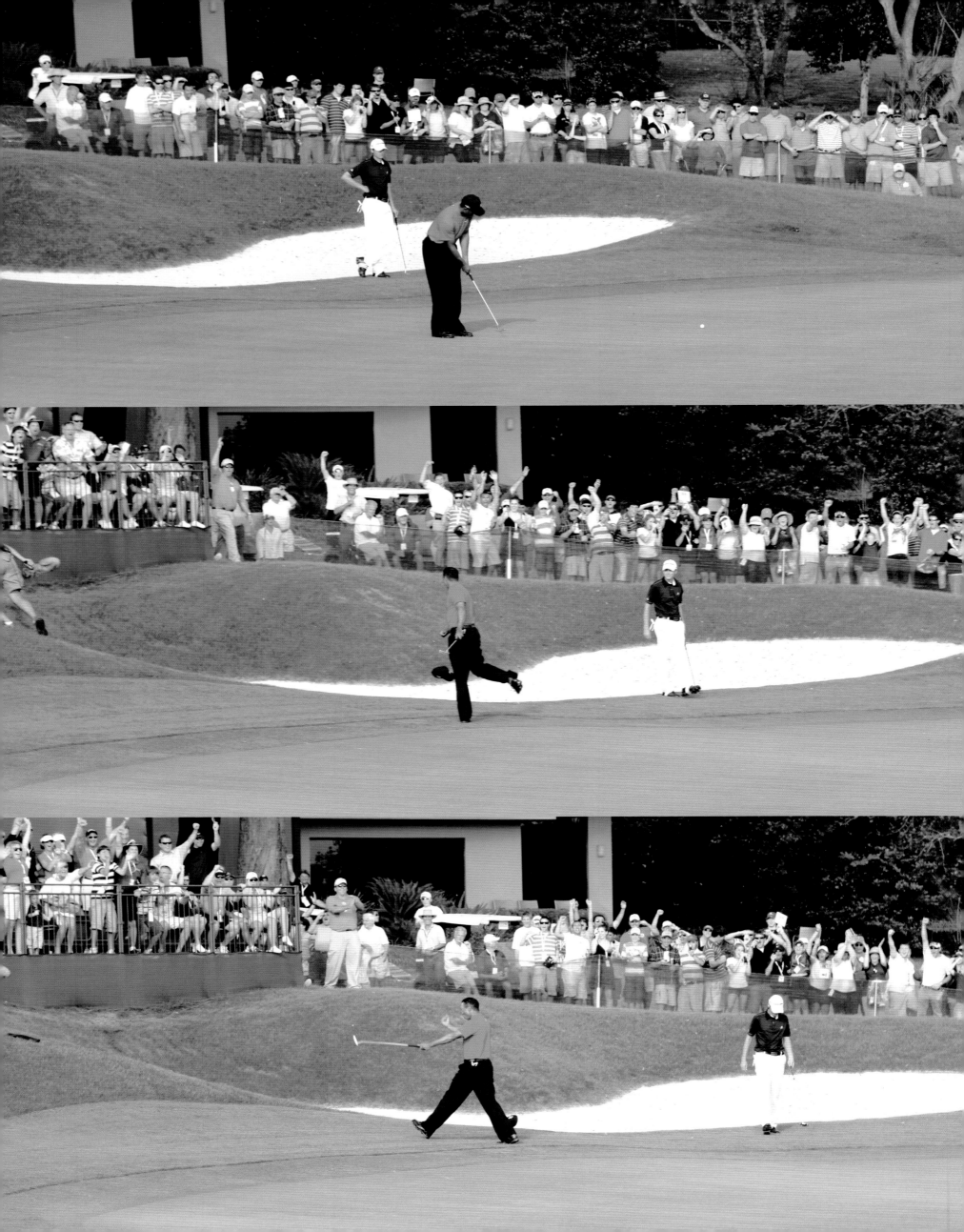

inches past the right side of the hole. Tiger got his par, and then hit a 4-iron into the fairway on the par-5 18th hole. He laid up, hit a wedge on the green, just missed his birdie putt, and tapped in to complete a bogey-free round at the U.S. Open.

"Weird ideas never crossed my mind, just because of the fact that I wanted to have a day where I made no bogeys," Tiger said. "That was my goal from the beginning of the day: No bogeys. And I think the highlight of—I don't want to say the highlight—but one of the biggest moments of the day was when I buried that putt on 16. I worked so hard not to make a bogey, and then I have a fifteen-footer for par. If I missed that putt, I would have been pissed at myself. I went up and buried that putt, and it felt so good to do that and then go on and get that up-and-down at 17. I figured I could handle 18."

Walking up the last fairway, Tiger told Williams that he had felt tranquil and at ease with himself all week. Four weeks later, Woods was in the final twosome of the British Open at the Old Course in St. Andrews, Scotland, playing with Duval. He had started the round six shots ahead of Duval and Thomas Bjorn. Duval had gotten within three shots of Tiger through seven holes, but Tiger was never really threatened. His only challenge came from the course down the back nine, and from himself. He wanted to hit *golf shots.*

On the par-5 14th hole, Tiger was 260 yards from the pin. He turned to Williams to discuss the shot. Williams suggested he aim for a spire on a church steeple in the town that was in view from where they stood. Tiger made a beautifully balanced swing and stared at the ball in flight as it came off the face of his 3-wood. It was flying directly toward the spire. Tiger looked at Williams and asked, "Is that what you wanted?"

Tiger has hit exactly the shot he wanted, and the shot required, so many times that one expects him to do just that. There's no deeper pleasure for me, as a golf writer, golfer, and golf-follower, than watching a player in command of himself, the ball, and the course. Standing just outside the wall that runs along the 18th fairway that Championship Sunday in 2000 at the Old Course, I had a clear view of Tiger on the tee. Spectators, including media, can't get on the actual holes at the Old Course during an Open. We're required to walk outside the boundaries of the course as it moves out from the clubhouse and then back towards town and the old gray edifice where resides The Royal and Ancient Golf Club of St. Andrews, which conducts the Championship. Tiger was cast in sharp relief on the 18th tee because there weren't any spectators around. He stood there, the Open Championship at hand. He was one hole away from winning his first Open Championship.

Tiger hit his tee shot on that last hole and stood there for a second, an imperious presence, and a golfing colossus. He made his way to his next shot and then to the last green. Tiger had followed his U.S. Open victory with a win in the British Open at the Old Course in St. Andrews. The next month he found himself in a three-hole playoff against Bob May

ARNOLD PALMER AND TIGER SHARE A LAUGH AT THE CLOSING CEREMONY
OF THE 2008 ARNOLD PALMER INVITATIONAL

at the PGA Championship. On the first playoff hole, the 16th, Tiger's putt from twenty-five feet was tracking for the hole, and he knew it. He started walking it in, then jogging it in, and he pointed at the ball as it fell in. This was yet another spontaneous Tiger performance.

Tiger had become the first golfer since Ben Hogan in 1953 to win three majors in one year. He wasn't done with wins in national Opens, or with grand shots and gestures. There was the 218-yard 6-iron that he hit from a fairway bunker, over a lake, on the last hole of

the 2000 Canadian Open at the Glen Abbey Golf Club in Oakville, Ontario. Tiger was one shot ahead of Grant Waite, with whom he was playing. Waite had already hit his second shot on the green of the par-5 and would surely make a birdie. He might even hole his putt for an eagle. Tiger studied his shot and picked the ball cleanly from the sand. The ball soared over the pond and finished thirty feet beyond the hole, just over the green. Waite and Tiger each birdied the hole, so Tiger won.

Then there was the moment when Tiger faced a fifteen-foot putt on the third extra hole of a sudden-death playoff against Ernie Els in the 2003 Presidents Cup in George, South Africa. Nicklaus, the U.S. captain, and Gary Player, the International captain, had chosen Tiger and Els to play off for the competition if it were tied after the matches ended. That had happened; now Tiger had to make this putt, which would force Els to hole a six-foot putt to extend the playoff. The result of the competition depended on what they did.

Tiger examined his putt in the fading light over the Links at Fancourt. He could barely see the line, but focused on the putt and made his stroke. As the ball neared the hole, Tiger

jabbed his right index finger toward the ball, which toppled in. "That was actually one of the most nerve-wracking moments I've ever had in golf," Tiger said. Nicklaus added, "No way in the world I'd have dreamed he'd make that putt." Els then made his putt to tie the hole. The competition was soon called on account of darkness, and the result declared a tie.

Tiger seems to hit memorable shots and makes decisive putts in nearly every tournament he plays. The possibility of making such shots and putts excites Woods, impresses his fellow players, and makes watching him nothing less than mandatory. Tiger's swing coach Hank Haney, with whom he has worked since March 2004, often says he's never seen a golfer with such a thirst for improvement, or one who can assimilate information as quickly. Are we not considering the nature of genius when we are thinking about Woods? Whether we are considering a golfer, a musician, a dancer, or another athlete in another sport—or anybody who is a genius in his or her creative art—we are aware of a profound talent to make something happen, and to let it happen. Genius is transformative in all kinds of ways and

makes a person feel it's possible to stretch himself or herself. Watching Tiger hit a golf ball, I want to rush to the practice range to work on my own game. We are compelled by genius, and feel elevated when we expose ourselves to it at the same time that we are aware of its abiding mysteries. The mystery that is Tiger Woods—and that Jules captures on film so that we may ponder it—is evident in so many decisive moments.

To another such moment, then. Tiger was behind the 16th green in the final round of the 2005 Masters. He held a 1-shot lead over Chris DiMarco, with whom he was playing. DiMarco had hit his tee shot on the par-3 hole fourteen feet below the pin. "There's a good chance he doesn't get this inside DiMarco's ball," CBS commentator Lanny Wadkins said. Woods couldn't hit his shot anywhere near a direct line to the hole, because of the slope. But he saw a spot twenty feet left of the hole. The ball landed where he saw it land, and then rolled ever so slowly to the right, finally hesitating on the lip before toppling in.

"It's one of the best shots I've ever hit because of the turning point involved," Tiger said after he beat DiMarco in a playoff. "If Chris makes his putt and I make bogey, all of a sudden I'm one back." He said he was hoping only for a "makeable" putt. He made the shot.

Flash forward nearly three years. Tiger had a thirty-five-foot birdie putt on the last green to win the 2008 Arnold Palmer Invitational at the Bay Hill Club in Orlando. The putt broke sharply left to right. He started moving back and to his left as the ball took the slope and neared the hole. As it fell, he whipped off his cap and flung it on the ground with his right hand. When Steve Williams handed his cap back to him, he wondered what had happened to make him lose it. Tiger hadn't realized he had thrown his cap. He was that into the decisive moment.

Then there was this, on the 18th hole of the third round of the 2008 U.S. Open at the South Course of the Torrey Pines Golf Club. Tiger could normally reach the par-5 easily in two shots. But he was playing in severe pain because of damage to his left knee, and what he would divulge later was a double stress fracture in that leg. Tiger knew he couldn't make a conventional swing to hit a long drive on the hole. He elected to hit a gigantic slice and found the fairway. He would have hit no more than a 4-iron for his next shot, but he couldn't make the swing he wanted, and so took a 5-wood and hit another massive slice. The ball started at ten o'clock and finished at two o'clock, settling some forty-five feet behind the hole. Tiger made the eagle putt. He stood there as the ball dropped, the picture of determination. He had moved himself into the final twosome with Rocco Mediate in the last round.

And then this happened: Tiger had to—absolutely had to—make a fifteen-foot birdie putt on the 72nd green at Torrey Pines to get into a Monday playoff with Mediate. The green was bumpy. Even if he hit a pure putt, the bumpy ground could knock it off line. But he could only control the stroke he made. Tiger studied the putt and stood behind the ball for longer than he usually takes. It was as if he were telling himself he could only control what he could control: the kind of stroke he made, contact, hitting the ball on the line he chose. If he could do that, he could accept what happened. He hit the pure putt he meant to hit. The ball wobbled as it progressed. The ball fell. Tiger fist-pumped and fist-pumped and fist-pumped. Elation. Job well done.

"Unbelievable," Mediate said. "I knew he'd make it. I knew it."

Tiger won the Monday playoff, which was scheduled for 18 holes but went one extra hole. He had again defined what was possible. He had reconstructive knee surgery eight days later. His season was over. He had ended it with a performance for the ages.

Performance. Photography. Tiger Woods. Jules Alexander. Golf can be a beautiful game, and it is never more so than when Tiger is in full flow and expressing himself through it. How lucky we are to be here now, in the Tiger Woods era. By following him and studying him, and through Jules' dynamic photography, we come nearer to understanding and appreciating his genius.

A WILL TO WIN

BY DAMON HACK

THE WORLD SEES ONLY the finished product, the Tiger Woods who lashes at a golf ball like Zeus throwing thunderbolts, the golfer who can extract brilliance from fairways and buried lies, the golfer who is at his most calm when the gallery and the writers and the marshals and the competitors are biting their nails to nubs.

On windy links and manicured greens, from golf's birthplace in Scotland to its temple in Augusta, Tiger Woods has forever changed the idea of what someone can do with a dimpled ball and a crooked stick.

Take the highest qualities of those before him and Woods has a piece of all of them: Hogan's ethos, Nicklaus' mind, Palmer's flair, Player's doggedness, Ballesteros' imagination, Jones' splendor.

"You would think going to the first tee that he would feel the pressure because everybody is expecting him to win, and it's the exact opposite," Chris DiMarco, one of Woods' rivals, once said. "The guy playing with him feels the most pressure. It's almost like he comes into his comfort zone in that situation and just relishes the fact that everybody, for the most part, wants to see him trip. People are like, 'Please make bogeys,' and he just puts the hammer down."

From his earliest days as a tot in glasses and oversized caps in Southern California, Woods has stepped onto a golf course wanting to beat it and everyone on it.

OPPOSITE PAGE: 2006 PLAYERS CHAMPIONSHIP; TPC AT SAWGRASS, JACKSONVILLE, FLORIDA

'He has pounded his sneakers on hotel treadmills and run the back streets of old country roads, forever changing the look of the golfer and, even more, the game itself."

Rudy Duran, who coached Tiger as a young child, remembers seeing Woods swing a golf club for the first time and not believing his eyes. His move, Duran said, was that of a miniature professional.

Woods' high school coach, Don Crosby, said that his will to be great was evident in every endeavor, whether hitting a golf ball or studying a foreign language.

During his years at Stanford and as an amateur, the world began to discover what we all realize now, that Woods may wield the kind of genius the game has never known.

Surely, Woods is not the only golfer with access to high-tech equipment and swing monitors and world-class instruction. He definitely wasn't the first infant to watch his parent swing a club.

What separates Tiger Woods from everyone else is that every atom, neuron, and strand of his DNA points him toward winning golf tournaments.

Inside the ropes, we see the symphony, the crescendos on the tee box and the green. We marvel at the ball at the base of a bunker flying more than 200 yards and landing safely by the flagstick.

Watch his club accelerate, decelerate, and accelerate again, crashing into the backside of the ball in a way that, somehow, even still today, sounds a little bit different than everyone else.

We have seen an 8-shot win at St. Andrews, a 12-shot victory at the Masters, and a 15-shot win at the U.S. Open at Pebble Beach.

We remember his first PGA Tour win in 1996 when he was skinny as a string bean, and the breathless television reporter asked him if he could have ever imagined winning a tournament so quickly.

Yes, Woods said, he really could.

But maybe it is what we don't see that really defines Woods, the golfer in his quieter moments, awake at four a.m. for a morning jog or a sprint in the afternoon heat or just one more trip to the weight room.

ABOVE: 2007 MEMORIAL TOURNAMENT; MUIRFIELD VILLAGE GOLF CLUB, DUBLIN, OHIO.
FOLLOWING PAGES: TIGER TEES OFF AT THE 2008 ARNOLD PALMER INVITATIONAL
AT BAY HILL CLUB & LODGE IN ORLANDO, FLORIDA

He has pounded his sneakers on hotel treadmills and run the back streets of old country roads, forever changing the look of the golfer and, even more, the game itself.

At the 2006 PGA Championship at Medinah, his final-round playing partner, Luke Donald, made the bold but foolhardy decision to match Sunday red shirts with him.

Donald may have been paying a tribute to his native England—the pants were white—but he seemed to shrink in stature standing next to Woods.

They would play head-to-head for four hours, yet the championship seemed over in five minutes.

"I didn't think anything of it," Woods said when asked about Donald's red shirt. "I thought it was kind of weird to have a blue belt with it."

The majors, the trophies, the plaudits, they all keep piling up for Woods. But it is important to remember that great achievements often come from humble beginnings.

In my only conversation with Woods' father, Earl, I asked him what made his son so impenetrable, so seemingly unaffected by any kryptonite.

He recalled the time when Woods was eleven-years-old, and the two had gone out for a round of golf in Southern California.

It was cold and miserable and raining sideways, and most of the carts were returning to the pro shop. The young Woods had made four birdies in his first five holes and wanted to keep playing. On they went, on an empty course, with Earl in his cart and Woods soaked to the bone and smiling.

"He's walking with his umbrella and his bag and his towel and his glove," Earl said. "He was happy as heck, never complaining. He shot a 67."

The 67s—and better—continue to stack up for Woods, the prodigy who has taken the game of golf by its roots, grabbed hard, and not stopped shaking it.

"Tiger was always taught, 'Play the golf course,' " Earl said. "He's not looking for excuses. He's not looking for guys to make mistakes. He's looking to beat the damn course."

A GOLF DAD'S SIMPLE GRATITUDE

BY JAMES DODSON

N THE SPRING 2001, I invited my son Jack to tag along with me to the annual Golf Writers of America Awards Dinner at the Masters. The PGA Tour player being honored that night was Tiger Woods.

Like the vast majority of my colleagues in attendance, it was impossible not to be impressed by the way Tiger Woods had so thoroughly taken command of the PGA Tour in just five seasons. During the 2000 season, for which he was being honored, for instance, he'd swept three of the four major championships and captured another six championships in such dominating fashion reporters had simply run out of superlatives to describe his play.

More interesting to me, however, and speaking more as a father than a reporter in an age when sports superstars tend to come and go like Roman candles in the backyard, and few if any appear to appreciate how their success impacts impressionable minds, I was favorably struck by the way this tall, engaging California kid with the 80-million-dollar Nike smile handled himself so adroitly in the public spotlight, with the press constantly clamoring for his attention, and a world of corporate expectations already resting on his youthful shoulders.

As it happened, my pint-sized dinner companion's admission ticket to the Masters that year came courtesy of Arnold Palmer, my own boyhood golf inspiration, whose memoirs I'd

recently helped craft. During the cocktail hour prior to the dinner, while I chatted with colleagues and solicited their thoughts about my next book project, I couldn't help but notice how Jack's eyes rarely strayed from the front doors of the Augusta Civic Center. He was the only kid in the hall that night, clearly conducting his own private Tigerwatch as he eagerly awaited the triumphant arrival of his hero.

When the big moment came, Tiger appeared dressed in a regal gray business suit, shaking hands and smiling all around, moving with the grace of a Roman gladiator, politely besieged by admiring men and women twice his age, a scene that widened Jack's eyes to the circumference of 19th hole drink coasters, as we watched the man of the hour pass within a few yards and begin to make his way into the crowded hall.

Fortunately, just before he passed through the doors, he glanced over and spotted Jack and turned in our direction, extending his hand to one startled and pleased ten-year-old fan.

I stepped back a few feet to give them a little breathing room, fumbling to open a new digital camera—thereby missing most of what they actually said to each other.

But whatever it was, Tiger quickly soon had Jack grinning and nodding vigorously.

Naturally, I asked if the honoree would consent to a quick photograph. "No problem," Tiger said and planted both hands on Jack's shoulders moments before I snapped the picture.

For Woods, this was just another brief encounter with an adoring young fan on his way into golf's modern pantheon. But for a young kid from Maine and his grateful old man, the moment held incalculable magic and perhaps a glimpse of worlds to come.

Not long afterward, I began researching Ben Hogan's extraordinary playing career and life, attempting to slip behind the flood-lit mystique of perhaps the most elusive and mythologized superstar in the history of American sports. If Arnold Palmer wore his emotions in gloriously plain view of the world, providing photographers and wordsmiths of his era with a bounty of insights into the yeoman forces that unleashed Arnie's Army, his predecessor Hogan carried his magic like a sorcerer's amulet hidden beneath folds of woolen gray, demanding the patience and diligence of a skilled archeologist to decipher the source of his power. As Jules Alexander's extraordinary photographs of Hogan at his peak

2008 ACCENTURE MATCH PLAY CHAMPIONSHIP; THE GALLERY AT DOVE MOUNTAIN, MARANA, ARIZONA

powerfully attest, however, The Hawk possessed what the old Hollywood glamour photographers liked to call "It"—some elusive but unmistakable lens "magic" that set him miles apart from his contemporaries, a kinetic energy field even the most rudimentary golf fan could feel like a psychic breeze as the "Garbo of Golf" passed along the fairways from mortal to legend.

Not too surprisingly, Hogan was perhaps the last great American athlete who looked most natural photographed in black and white. Palmer, on the other hand, sporting Creamsickle sweaters and a Gary Cooper smile, was the perfect creature for a media age exploding with living color—just the guy to bring golf into the dens and living rooms of Middle America.

After nearly a decade now of watching Tiger Woods perform his own form of magic in professional golf, I've come to think of him as something of a splendid fusion of Hogan and Palmer, entirely original in his own style and presentation, to be sure, but unmistakably possessing key elements of both his legendary predecessors in the way he can summon forth greatness at the critical moment with a concentration eerily recalling that of The Hawk, yet visually dazzle the galleries and delight his fans with outbursts of raw emotion that vault the game to breathtaking heights exactly the way Arnie did at the peak of his playing prowess.

Speaking more as grateful golf papa than game historian on the subject of Tigermania,

A VIEW THROUGH THE LENS

I took these photos at the 216-yard, par-3 16th hole at Muirfield Village Golf Club in Dublin, Ohio. Tiger's playing partner was Steve Jones, winner of the U.S. Open at Oakland Hills. Tiger's tee shot was headed into the trees and possibly out of bounds; however, it hit a limb and bounced back onto the green about twelve feet from the hole. The crowd erupted with cheers and cries of "You're so lucky, Tiger!" Jones laughed and agreed with the fans. Tiger responded to all this with a sheepish grin and went on to make the putt. A good time was had by all.   —*Jules Alexander*

A VIEW THROUGH THE LENS

In the photo at left, I photographed Tiger teeing off on the first hole during the first round of the 2006 U.S. Open Championship at Winged Foot Golf Club in Mamaroneck, New York. It was almost 47 years to the day that I photographed Ben Hogan on the first hole during the first round of the 1959 U.S. Open at the same historic venue, not far from my home. Being there at the tee certainly brought back memories. Note that the yardage of the hole has increased by only eight yards.

The small boy with his mother in the photo below contacted me in 1995 when he saw this photo in my book, *The Hogan Mystique*. I glady sent him a print.

—*Jules Alexander*

as professional golf has increasingly become a big-money affair dominated by major corporate influences and support teams of swing coaches and psychologists, diminishing the footprints of colorful characters in the game, I've been pleased to note how Tiger Woods, for all his worldly success, remains something of a big kid when it comes to playing the game.

For what it's worth, I contend this visible youthful passion—which one moment produces a dazzling smile and the next an expletive not-quite-so-deleted—is central to the vast popular appeal, and growing legend, of Tiger Woods.

In our household, Tigermania crept unobtrusively through the door around the start of the New Millennium, when, on any given weekend, my young son began casually poking his head into the den anytime golf was on TV to inquire, "So how's Tiger doing?" If I reported that Tiger was on or somewhere near the lead, especially in a major championship, young Jack immediately abandoned whatever he was up to and planted himself directly in front of the tube to catch the action.

A short time later, he took up playing the game wearing a red shirt and Nike spikes, even copying his hero's exuberant air-punches and other stylish mannerisms on the golf course—not unlike the way his old man once upon a time copied the knock-kneed putting stance and corkscrew swing of his favorite fairway action hero, Arnold Palmer.

Ironically, during two summer research expeditions to Fort Worth, Texas, while I attempted to excavate the well-hidden life of one William Ben Hogan, Jack spent a couple weeks out at Hank Haney's Golf Ranch refining his exuberant golf swing under a fellow who would soon become Wood's own golf coach.

By the time Jack reached junior high school, he was attempting to organize a school golf team and talking about some day becoming a golf pro like his hero. By the time he made his high school golf team, more than one astute observer could even see unmistakable traces of Tiger Woods in his nicely evolving golf swing.

As I write this, Jack is preparing to begin his final high school golf season, playing first or second man on a team that might well contend for the state high school golf championship. Curiously, though, he not longer speaks of playing the game professionally—and maybe not even in college. He plays the game strictly for the pleasure of beating his buddies and the glory of his school, the joy of chasing Old Man Par. Someday very soon, he'll even beat his old man.

For the record, nothing could please his old man more than that. With it's swing gurus and solemn faces, pro golf simply ain't what it used—but, luckily, Tiger Woods is. Like Hogan and Palmer before him, as Jules Alexander's photo documentary of his splendid career thus far handsomely reveals, Tiger Woods clearly has "It," too.

Since that brief encounter in the lobby of the old Augusta Civic Center, Jack has grown as tall and broad-shouldered as his first great sports hero, while Woods has gone on to claim sixty-five official PGA titles and fourteen major championships.

He has blown past Hogan and Palmer, and in all likelihood will completely rewrite the

2006 ARNOLD PALMER INVITATIONAL, 6TH HOLE; BAY HILL CLUB & LODGE, ORLANDO, FLORIDA

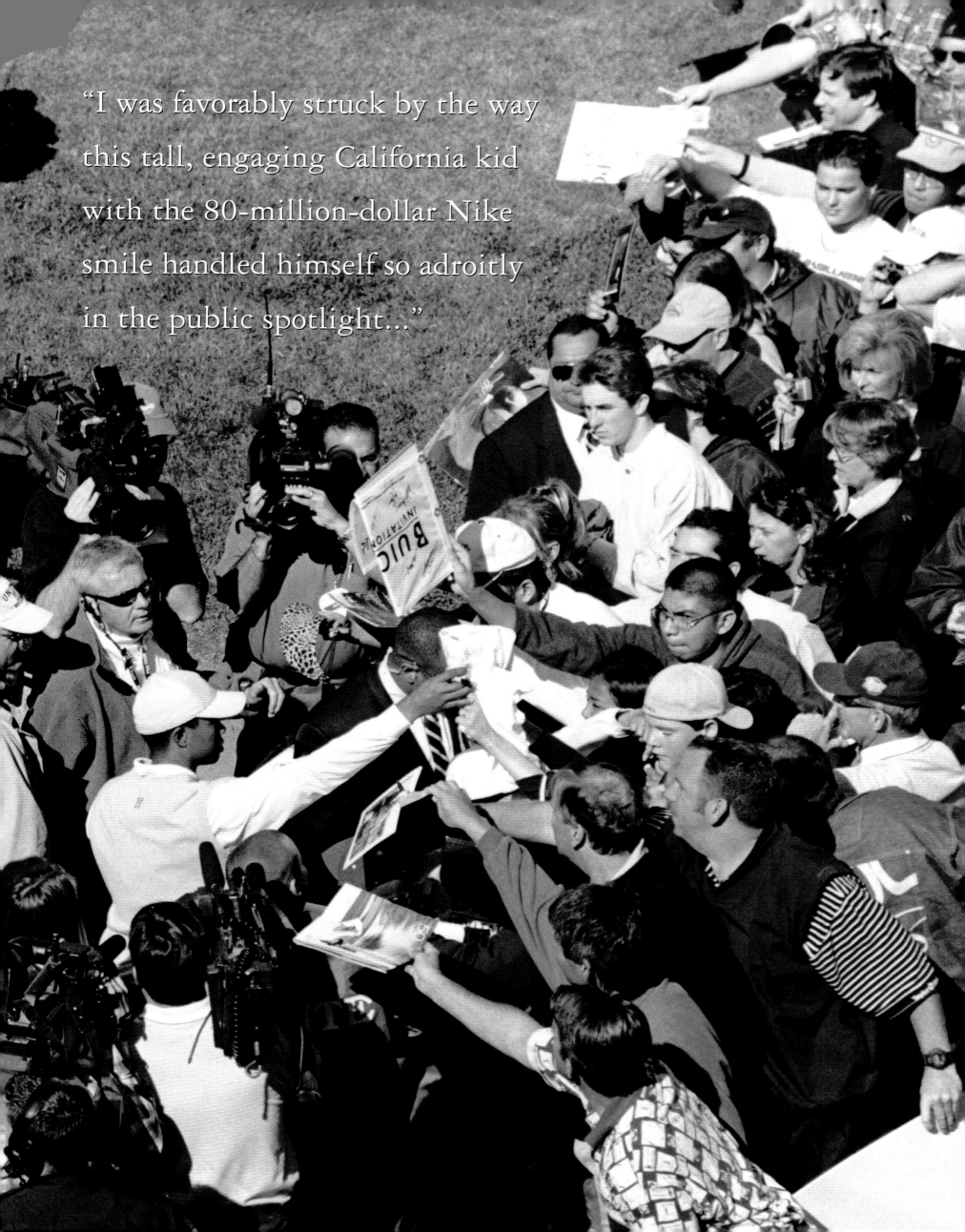

"I was favorably struck by the way this tall, engaging California kid with the 80-million-dollar Nike smile handled himself so adroitly in the public spotlight..."

PGA Tour record books before he's finished. His influence on the game and future generations of golfers may prove as irresistible and unforgettable as his Sunday red shirt.

And he even became a father.

I'm sure, in that regard, he'd completely understand my paternal gratitude to him for being such an excellent role model for a wide-eyed kid from Maine—and a blue million other kids everywhere.

His picture, after all, still sits on Jack's desk. Both of them are frozen in time, grinning like two kids sharing a big secret about tomorrow.

PHOTOGRAPHER'S NOTE To my dear father, who put a camera in my hands when I was twelve-years-old. To my wife Danna, who encouraged me for forty years. To my sons Paul and Carl, who urged me to keep shooting and to join the 21st century. And to my jazz musician brother, who took me to Swing Street in New York City to photograph Benny Goodman, Frank Sinatra, Duke Ellington, and others while I was still in high school. Thanks to all of the magazine editors, art directors, and clients that trusted me over the years. And thanks to the people that believed in me and supported me from the start, specifically, Michael Ainslie, who was with me all the way on this project, as well as Ken Natori, Larry Hasak, and folks at the PGA Tour. Also to Golf House; The World Golf Hall of Fame; George Peper; Matt Ginella of *Golf Digest*; Charlie Robson of the Metropolitan Golf Association; Darrek Robertson, my occasional assistant, Chris Millard, and Barry Hyde of the USGA. To Aaron Schechter, my friend since grade school, my confidant and my advisor for so many years. And I have to express my gratitude for the recognition that my book *The Hogan Mystique* brought to me. On this book, *Tiger Woods In Black & White*, I owe my thanks to my essay writers, Jim Nantz, Dave Anderson, Damon Hack, James Dodson, and Lorne Rubenstein, who each wrote such wonderful pieces, along with Johnny Miller for his insightful commentary. And finally, to the staff at Hasak Inc., who put it all together.

—*Jules Alexander*

TIGER WITH DAUGHTER SAM AFTER HIS VICTORY AT THE 2008 U.S. OPEN
AT TORREY PINES, LA JOLLA, CALIFORNIA